THE
FIVE STEPS
OF THE SALE

How to Sell and Close 99% MORE in your Presentation

Paul R. Atkinson, CPC

ARCHWAY
PUBLISHING

Archway Publishing books may be ordered
through booksellers or by contacting:

Archway Publishing
1663 Liberty Drive
Bloomington, IN 47403
www.archwaypublishing.com
844-669-3957

Because of the dynamic nature of the Internet, any web addresses or
links contained in this book may have changed since publication and
may no longer be valid. The views expressed in this work are solely those
of the author and do not necessarily reflect the views of the publisher,
and the publisher hereby disclaims any responsibility for them.

Any people depicted in stock imagery provided by Getty Images are
models, and such images are being used for illustrative purposes only.
Certain stock imagery © Getty Images.

For information and courses contact:

Positive Mental Attitudes
6750 N. Andrews Ave, Suite 200
Fort Lauderdale, Florida, 33309
www.paulratkinson.com
Call or text: 954-461-1786

Edited by
Rajiv Bee

Illustrations by
Gregorio Semon Jr.
GoDaddy Social

ISBN: 978-1-6657-2040-3 (sc)
ISBN: 978-1-6657-2041-0 (e)

Library of Congress Control Number: 2022904998

Print information available on the last page.

Archway Publishing rev. date: 04/11/2022

Contents

Thank you

My greatest gratitude to my heavenly father GOD, for giving me so many decades in using this technique. With this I have touched so many lives, enriching people to achieve their goals, wants and needs.

Now I share this system with you and pray you benefit even more than I have.

Introduction

There is no dearth of people who begin their professional journeys without realizing that they need to possess a vital element. This skill set holds the key to what might result in monumental success, day after day, month after month, quarter after quarter, and year after year. This crucial element determines our growth and end results, no matter which career we choose.

The element I'm talking about, dear readers, is selling. The vital skill set that enables you to sell makes you a superior and masterful salesperson who wins each day.

What does selling mean to you? Some might say it's closing a deal or getting someone to buy from you. While that's correct, to me, there's more to selling. It involves following a systematic method and getting your prospects to close on their own accord. In essence, you need them to wholeheartedly believe what you're offering is exactly what they want and need. This sales technique takes prospects on a journey and leads them right into closing deals with you.

Does it sound amazing? Well, I'll let you answer that. In my case, though, I've been using this system since 1993, to sell just about anything you can think of. The system is fun, vibrant, precise, logical, and, among other things, easy to learn.

Learning and using this selling system helps us to be in complete control of all our sales processes from beginning to end. While it makes us comfortable, it also makes our prospects just as comfortable, all throughout its five steps. If all you do is follow these steps, the system will always lead the prospect to close with you.

This sales system is called The Five Steps of the Sale. It is remarkable and life-changing. Once you start implementing it, it will show you a new way of life in which closing deals will become second nature. After you start using this system with your prospects, you'll become their favorite salesperson in quick time.

No matter what product or service you have to offer, get ready to increase your sales closings by up to 10 times once you start using The Five Steps of the Sale. In most examples and contexts, I use a real estate selling environment or atmosphere to get the point across. All you need to do is place yourself and your career or product in its place to understand the point.

Let's go Sell em Tiger!

Welcome to the Five Steps of the Sale

SALES ARE WHAT WE WANT PLENTY OF WHEN OUR WORK involves selling something. Selling is a skill set you need to embrace if you hope for prospective clients to close with you. If you lack this skill, chances are you will not make many sales.

Why do you need to be able to sell? Have you ever met salespersons you did not like or found pushy or ones who did not listen to you or had no idea about what you really wanted? Sure, you have because they exist all over the place. Much like you, I cannot stand to be around such salespeople. I will not buy from anyone who fits this bill. Instead, I'll find a salesperson I like and connect with to make my purchase or agreement.

If your work requires you to close deals so you may put bread on the table, it's pertinent that you have good selling skills. If you don't, hardships tend to follow.

The pages ahead offer valuable insight surrounding the selling technique I've used with great results for around three decades now. It is to this I owe all the sweet and enjoyable journeys of being the top salesperson in all my sales roles.

I've sold for the US Navy and to high school students; I've sold cars, insurance, computers, and credit card machines. And then there's my favorite—selling real estate. Using and mastering the system over the years has granted me the comfort and pleasure of a successful career in sales. The life I lead now is happy, rewarding, and abundant, and I leave enormous wealth for generations to come.

After years of practicing and mastering my system, I now pass it on to you. Let your new, unparalleled, unrelenting, and flawless sales career journey begin with *The Five Steps of the Sale.*

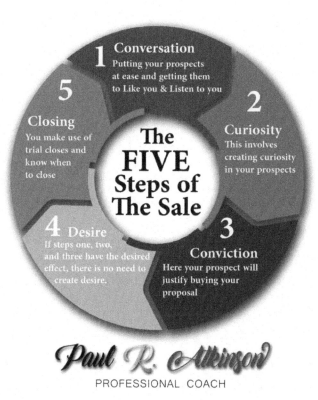

The FIVE Steps of The Sale

1 Conversation
Putting your prospects at ease and getting them to Like you & Listen to you

2 Curiosity
This involves creating curiosity in your prospects

3 Conviction
Here your prospect will justify buying your proposal

4 Desire
If steps one, two, and three have the desired effect, there is no need to create desire.

5 Closing
You make use of trial closes and know when to close

Paul R. Atkinson
PROFESSIONAL COACH

Let's go sell 'em, tiger!

Why Use the Five Steps of the Sale?

THE SIMPLE ANSWER IS THAT ONCE YOU KNOW HOW TO use the system, it will empower you by giving you mastery in selling.

I feel providing some background information might help before getting started. I spent over fourteen years in the US Navy, and I am proud and grateful to have served this country. During that time, I worked as a recruiter. I wanted to sell a career in the navy to anyone who'd lend me an ear. However, I was quick to find out that I wasn't cut out for selling. I did not know how to close or get a prospect to sign up.

That, of course, was until I figured out that there was a much simpler way to get people to join. After I started using the five steps of the sale process, I became the top recruiter for seven consecutive years.

In 2003 I started my sales career as a real estate agent. The day I received my real estate license, I closed my first sale. On the very first day, I wrote a contract with a husband and wife, the buyers. The seller accepted the offer the next day. That's the effectiveness of the five steps of the sale.

During my career as a real estate agent, I have continued to generate more income each year. At the time of completing this book, I have accounted for more than $82 billion in sales volume by using this technique. I'm now going to show you just how to learn it, practice it, and let it become a part of you.

What you'll see unfold is a systemic approach that goes in steps one through five. Each step brings your prospects closer and closer to closing deals on their own.

Bear in mind that it's very important for you to understand each step completely before moving on to the next. If not, you will miss the markers and not close. The only step you may get to bypass is the fourth (desire). This is because when you get the first three right, you'll move directly to the fifth.

What Do You Need?

You'll need some tools to develop your skills through the five steps. Think about anything that's been created or completed well—it obviously took planning and use of some tools.

As you read through, be very aware that this systematic approach will help you become an exceptional salesperson. When you follow my guidance and pay attention to the details you're about to discover, not only will you look at life through a different perspective but you will also begin to see an increase in your closings immediately. The faster you get this under your belt and begin to use it, the sooner you will begin to enjoy a wonderful professional and personal life.

The Right Perception

When you look at all that's required, the first thing that stands out is the fact that you must have the right perception. Simply put, perception refers to the organization, identification, and interpretation of sensory information in the human brain. This helps an individual understand and represent his or her environment.

Not that simply put, you say? Well, this story should clear things up.

It goes back to the time when I was in the US Navy. I had just started recruiting and got a government car to drive around town. The navy also gave me a credit card for expenses as well as a cell phone, so I didn't have to use my own. Then they said, "Get out there into the city, Camden, New Jersey, and start to recruit."

Before I left, they gave me a warning, saying, "Hey, perception becomes one's own reality. You need to make sure when you're wearing this uniform, people perceive you as one of the top recruiters for the United States right here inside of the community."

What did they say? They said, "Perception becomes one's own reality." You must know that one of the most important tools you need to have is the right perception. How does your community see you as the top real estate agent or as that top businessperson?

Dressing and Professionalism

Do you dress professionally? Do you look and behave professionally? Are you creating an effective perception of your brand? Where is it that you're going to sell? For instance, if you wish to sell on the beach, wearing Tommy Bahama clothing is just fine. It's fine because you will blend well with all the beachgoers. What if you're to sell properties in a golfing community?

Understand that this aspect correlates to your market. If you want to sell luxury homes, make sure you have a few good suits and an otherwise impeccable-looking wardrobe so you're always dressed to the *T*.

Believe it or not, looking professional is an integral part of your selling skills. It gives you the ability to be liked and to be listened to just because of your appearance. Once people like you and feel that they can communicate with you openly, they will be more receptive in listening to what you have to say. This ability to be liked and listened to comes from dressing and behaving professionally, which makes them very important tools.

Ability to Gain Trust

While you must have the ability to be trusted, how do you go about the process? You do this by giving the people you interact with the information they need and empowering them. I'll show you just how to build trust with your prospects a little later in the book.

Ability to Read the Playing Field

What does reading the playing field mean? When you step into an environment during your sales process and see and analyze things around you, how do you read the situation so you know what to say or what to talk about? I'm going to show you how to do just that through the five steps as well.

Ability to Use Association and Mirror Techniques

Another vital tool you need in your arsenal is the ability to use association and mirroring techniques. The association technique refers to the ability of associating topics and items with others, and I'll show you how to do this in the pages to come.

With the mirroring technique, you use actions and behaviors of others to connect with them instantly and in a fruitful manner. I will give you a few examples of how to connect with your prospects very quickly a little later.

When you use both these techniques, you'll discover just how you can get someone to listen to you and like you in as little as fifteen seconds. That's wonderful, right? Have you heard about these techniques before? There's no need to worry if you haven't because I will show you just how to use these effectively.

The Right Mindset: the Nuclear Mind

When we're in the process of selling something, a lot of chatter tends to clutter our minds. Do you carry little crumbs of doubts, thinking even for a minute, that a sale might not happen? Do you feel prospects might not sign with you, but that you'll try anyway? Unless your answer is a resounding no, understand that you cannot carry on with this mindset. If you hope to succeed at selling, all your thoughts need to be positive (with a capital *P*, if you may).

During the early 1990s, I discovered a way to keep my mind in check at all times, down to every minute of the day. This technique has allowed me to control my mind, and thereby, my behaviors, actions, and motivation. Can you imagine having something in your tool bag that gives your mind a boost as and when needed and helps you pull through any circumstance in life, be it personal or professional?

In today's world, a significant percentage of the human population comes without a strong mindset. However, if you want to be a top-selling salesperson in your field of choice, you must have the right mindset, or what I refer to as "the nuclear mind." We will delve deeper into this as you continue reading.

Practice

The most important tool and the final piece of the puzzle involves practice, practice, and some more practice. Well, I have been practicing The Five Steps of the Sale system since 1993. Yes, practicing. To become a master salesperson who closes 90% and more of the time, you must gain mastery in The Five Steps of the Sale, and this comes only through rigorous practice.

> *"Practice what you know, and it will help to make clear what now you do not know."*
> *Rembrandt*

The Nuclear Mind - Going Deeper

A nuclear mind is self-starting and self-generating. It has a constant supply of power and strength. Most importantly, a nuclear mind repairs and restores itself with a governing methodology. Simply put, the nuclear mind is atomic. It achieves, leads, teaches, understands, wastes no time, delegates, and dispositions. Having said this, how do we develop a nuclear mind?

You need to make a few changes in your daily routine. Begin each day with a purpose. Start your day with a plan already outlined from the day before. Never wake up without a plan for the day already in place.

Have your calendar set with tasks that make for a balanced day. This includes giving time to your health, family, spirituality, and career. Every day needs to incorporate all four elements as they contribute to your core balance.

Let us begin with health. Set a time to get your daily quota of exercise, whether it is a walk, a run, a swim, a workout class, or just stretches. Give your body that endorphin kicker it needs. Do you know that endorphins work in reducing pain and cause feelings of pleasure and euphoria? If you find this unbelievable, take a look in the dictionary.

During my association with the military for fourteen years, workouts were part of my everyday life. We always began each day with exercise. No sooner than we were up, we dressed for exercise and got it done. Not many of us can push this through, I say for sure. However, if you make this happen, it will take you to a place you have never been in your business.

Next, set a time for your family in your calendar. This may seem simple, and you may think you are good and don't need to write it down. However, think of managing multiple tasks every day. Failing to keep a tab on all that you need to do in a centralized location, for your support system to access, is not beneficial to your balance or growth. You will leave something out if you don't have it all in plain sight.

Make a note of that lunch with your significant other, your child's game that you need to attend, dinner plans with the family, or even a call to say, "I'm thinking of you." These breaks in between events boost your drive toward the next task at hand, and they keep you rooted and grounded in your family's love.

Think of how your family and friends feel when you include them in your everyday life in this manner. What becomes of it? What about you? How amazing will you feel knowing you did not skip a beat of the drum you're playing?

Spirituality gives you that all-important solid ground to step on each day. You may read books, listen to podcasts, or watch videos to take you there – to a place where you feel self-centered and at ease, and believe in your hopes and dreams. Chip away at it every day without fail.

Most of the times when I do this, I discover my word for the day. It opens my eyes to the true meaning of life and sets my mind on the path for that day. It's a must-have for me, and once you involve yourself in the process, it will be for you too. Look at what your spirituality is and define it in your own way. Get suitable resources on your devices that you may easily access while lying in your bed before your feet hit the ground.

Your career, of course, is the core of it all in producing income. We have to provide for ourselves and our family. Know your work well. Make the most of your skills and knowledge, and incorporate a productive daily plan that will take you one step further in achieving your mission or vision for the day. Again, you chip away at it.

Let's say your goal is to make $100,000 in the next year. You need to break it down into manageable moments. Divide that amount by four to get your quarterly goals. Divide the quarterly goals by three for your monthly goal. Then, divide your monthly goal by the number of days you plan to contribute toward work in that month.

For example, an annual goal of $100,000 results in $25,000 per quarter. Per month, the figure stands at $8,333. Divide the $8,333 by 22 working days, which basically means that you need to produce or make $379 per day for the planned month.

Some days you may double or triple the goal of $379, and that puts you ahead. Even then, don't let up. Keep pushing to make the month a success in your monthly plan. Enjoy the days you don't work. Restore your mind and body. In doing so, your next day to work will be on point, impactful, and powerful.

A nuclear mind needs your support with all of the above – a calendar that is incorporated with tasks for health, family, spirituality, and career. This is the secret recipe for making your mind nuclear. Realize that you will have to chip away at each task, every day. Rome, after all, was not built in a day. It happened slowly, but surely.

Imagine you want to build a four-foot tall brick wall, and you have a pile of bricks. You rise up every day, get ready, and begin work. You take bricks, one by one, and put them in place, day after day. Eventually, you see a four feet tall brick wall right before your eyes.

You use what you need and ensure that you do your part to reinforce the wall with what it requires to keep standing strong. Chip away at it, I say. The systems you use and the growth that follows will be noticed, and this gives you the ability to produce for many more years to come.

As you become proficient in this way of life, you discover how you can begin to stack your tasks. Stacking, for the experienced, makes time to do and achieve more. What am I saying? Consider this – you begin your day with a run, along with a family member, while you're also listening to your spiritual input for the day. Do you notice that this one task incorporates health, family, and spirituality? Is that not amazing?

Here is another example, where your typical workday involves interacting and working with people, and the networking bringing an increase in business. You may choose to invite a prospect for dinner with his or her significant other, and you include your better half into the plan as well. This way, you spend time having a great meal with your loved one, while also getting to bond with your prospect.

Stacking is incorporating a task with allowable events that contribute to more than one aspect of your core balance. Master each core in its own realm at first. Then, begin to see how you may stack to gain extra room in your day to achieve more. It's nothing less than amazing when you get in the flow.

There is a formula to use when creating a Nuclear Mind, you will see it ahead shortly. First, you must check your mood meter and ask yourself what you are feeling at the moment. Second, say your mantra. Third, regulate your thoughts. Think only positive thoughts to counter the negative thoughts in your mind. Finally, take action and jump to your feet immediately.

What you also need is your own mantra. The dictionary definition of mantra is, "a word or sound repeated to aid concentration in meditation; or a statement or slogan repeated frequently."

I discovered my mantra in the mid-1990s. It goes, "I am the world's best presenter. I am persuasive and am compelling."

What is yours? Find it and keep saying it repeatedly. Say it before a meeting, before a workout, while working out, while getting ready, and at any time you feel a little lack of something. Stop and think what your mantra can be now and write it down. Become one with it, and let it become you. You need it for your journey.

The Nuclear Mind

THE **NUCLEAR** MIND

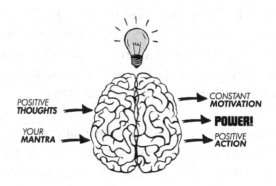

HERE IS THE NUCLEAR MIND FORMULA. APPLY IT TO your daily routine over the next thirty days and see how you transform.

30-Day Plan for Creating a Nuclear Mind

A Nuclear Mind = Check Your Mood Meter + Say Your Mantra + Regulate Your Thoughts + Take Action

A nuclear mind has all the characteristics of a tiger. It is strong, vibrant, powerful, fearless, and courageous. Develop a nuclear mind and see how good you become at formulating your goals and achieving them in a sustained manner.

***The Pusher. "Today I will be the master
of my emotions!" - Og Mandino***

Once you have the Nuclear Mind concept and formula down pat, it is very important that you go through the corresponding exercise every day. It helps enforce your new learning and solidifies the change that needs to happen. You can achieve this by using a technique I've devised. It's called Positive Expectation (PE).

PE is a mind changing tool and one that I've been using since the early 1990s. It works wonders. What it does is it helps you take a look at how you can change your mindset from negative thoughts to being completely positive all the time. All you need to do is follow my technique and go through the PE exercise every day, preferably first thing in the morning, before you engage with anyone else.

PE Exercise

1. Once you're up and awake, complete the Nuclear Mind formula before speaking with anyone.
2. Make a note of all the activities you have planned for the day ahead.
3. Close your eyes, take a deep breath, let it out, and relax.
4. Envision that your first activity, no matter what it is, will produce a positive outcome.
5. Next, envision the next activity to deliver a positive outcome.
6. Do this with all the activities you've listed.

7. Repeat this until you envision all your daily activities, no matter what they are, to produce positive outcomes.

8. Repeat steps one through seven every day for the next 90 days.

By completing this exercise regularly, you will quickly notice how everything in your life has started producing positive results. Your ability to use my technique that is fun, unique, and precise will make you among the top producing salespeople in your market.

As you move deeper into learning The Five Steps of The Sale, remember that you must take this vital required tool, PE, with you. Every day, before you get in front of everyone that you are going to sell, you must already have envisioned them listening to you, liking you, trusting you, curious to hear your proposal, loving your presentation, and then simply signing the dotted line with you and only you. Wow! This is hot stuff. All my secrets are now in the palms of your hands. Oh, Yeah!

Let's go sell em Tiger!

Step 1 - Conversation

WITHOUT FURTHER ADO, LET'S GET INTO THE MEAT OF the selling technique I love so much and use to close 99% of my sales. First, I want you to use all the required tools mentioned until now. Go over them once more to ensure you comprehend them well. Then, proceed to learn the five steps, one at a time.

Remember that every time you use this technique, you must use positive expectations and envision your presentations to produce successful outcomes all the time. Close your eyes right now. Imagine feeling blissful through a meeting and sense that happiness. See your client signing and feel like a champion because you just closed another sale.

In the first step, conversation, you get your prospects to like you, to listen to you, to trust you, and to believe in you. This is the stage where you discover their wants, their needs, and their dominant buying motive (DBM). The last aspect refers to how they end up feeling when they get what they want or need. All these aspects are vital in getting your prospect to the closing table, and I will define them as we continue.

Conversation makes use of a clear system, and not tactics, to get prospects where you want them to be. The method of recognizing personality type by using Tai Lopez's

P.A.S.E. system gives you the ability to build rapport in a matter of seconds.

P stands for Practical, suggesting that such a person is calculated, logical, and down to earth. Prospects may demonstrate this trait during your observation by prioritizing their work and thought processes. For instance, a prospect might maintain a logical order of things while displaying confidence and the ability to make decisions. They don't act without knowing what they are doing. Instead, they follow an order in which information must flow methodically. This, in turn, leads them to pull the trigger.

How can you tell if a prospect is a P-type personality? I do it by quickly analyzing conversations. Is a prospect asking me questions in a logical or orderly fashion to gain better understanding? When you make note of this in your conversations, you get to offer your prospect all the required information in a practical manner. Simply put, you give them the information they seek in a way they understand best. Once they see you're speaking their language, quick connections follow.

A is for Action, and people with this type of personality are typically action-based, aggressive, and fast. It's common for them to talk fast at times and paint pictures of getting to the end results in BOLD. A good example I come across often involves prospects pushing to get what they want and being overly eager in ensuring that things get done in the right manner.

In my field of work, they are quick to ask me to get the keys and show them the property they seek in haste, typically "today". They can ask you to call sellers and ask them if they would do something their way. You can spot this type of person right off the bat. Connecting with them is easy, just repeat what they say they want you to do. Ask them to give you some time so you may work on what's required.

Work on completing the task at hand as quickly as possible. Get back to them promptly; even if it's to inform them that what they're asking you to do is not possible based on what you've learned. Teach them how to move past what they are pushing for by educating them. They will immediately connect with you and appreciate your actions.

The S is for Social, implying that people with this trait talk a lot. They, as you may imagine, represent the social butterflies of our world. To me, they are very easy to spot and to connect with quickly. Just jump into conversations and lead them to you by using the tactics that you get to learn in the upcoming pages – the association and mirroring techniques.

The E stands for Emotional, and these people are typically sensitive. It should come as no surprise that they might cry or get teary-eyed at the drop of a hat. If you're telling them a story, you will be quick to see their emotions, be it being joyous, sad, or sympathetic.

When I notice this behavior in people during my sales process, I connect with them easily by tapping into my heart, my empathy, and my love for fellow human beings. You may also make these connections quickly by relying on what I refer to as psychological reciprocity.

This requires that you give your prospects credit for their beliefs, feelings, emotions, and/or values. They, in turn, become morally obligated to give you credit for your beliefs, feelings, emotions, and values. However, you need to ensure that you do not use sympathy to get the prospect to move in your direction or towards the closing. As with the other techniques, you'll get to understand this further a little later in this book.

When you get quick insight into the personality type of your prospect, you move to using the tactics I've mentioned earlier. You rely on the association technique, the mirroring technique, and psychological reciprocity to bond and connect with them. These tactics help address a prospect's fear and uncertainty quickly and effectively. Using these valuable tools gives you the ability to build rapport in a matter of seconds.

The Association Technique

Have you ever wondered how some salespeople are seemingly gifted when it comes to connecting with others instantly? When I learned of this many years ago, I discovered that this was a secret that the top producers did not even talk about. When asked how they do what they do, they would say, "Oh, you have to connect with your client first." That's it, and nothing more. Just how the heck do we connect with a client, though? You do it by using this technique and the two that follow.

The association technique is my favorite and the most commonly used. It helps you find something or things that get you to associate with your prospect. For example, when I engage with prospects, I can get them to like me and listen to me within the first 15 seconds by simply associating with something I see, hear, smell, taste, or feel.

How does this work? The moment you communicate with a prospect, ask yourself what common things you notice between you and him/her.

Decoding the answers to these 10 simple questions will help:

1. Is there a place that you have both visited, lived in, or know of?
2. Is there someone in common you both know?
3. Is there a type of clothing you both wear?
4. Is there an item you both own, or one that's owned by your prospect and someone you know?
5. Is there a song, an artist, a band, or a genre of music you both like?
6. Is there a common phrase both of you use?
7. Is there a common second language you both know?
8. Is there a smell that feels familiar to both?
9. Is there a taste you both love?
10. Is there a feeling you both share from a similar experience?

As soon as you find a way to associate with your prospect, grab it quickly and indulge in it for a few moments. When you're doing this, make sure you're relaxed. Be real, smile, and know that you're a human being with love in your heart. "Love them up," is what I always say. Get in the moment, forget about yourself, and take notice of what your prospects are saying and doing, as well as their body language. Make them relax and open, just as you are in that moment.

To really get this technique going, you'll have to begin using it in your everyday life. Here is an exercise that will point you in the right direction to mastering this.

Exercise 1

A. Go through the 10 questions listed just above at breakfast, lunch, and dinner. Do this at least three times each day, for three consecutive days.

B. On day four, after you have understood all the 10 questions well, take a close look at your next conversation and all that follows during the day. Identify all the associations through your interactions with other people.

C. When you find an association, take a deep breath, relax, and enjoy the conversation.

D. Then, show and tell the people you're interacting with that you are listening and paying attention to them through associations.

E. Get to a mental state where you feel and exude love through your conversation.

F. Repeat this entire exercise every day.

The Mirroring Technique

Much like the association technique that you may use to instantly connect with your prospects, so you may with the mirroring technique. This is equally fun and relaxing. However, if used incorrectly, you may find yourself in a tight spot with your prospect and it can result in hampering the rapport-building process.

Be very careful when using this technique. I strongly recommend completing the exercise that follows several times even before you try to test the waters. You should know, though, that this technique is very effective when connecting with people quickly.

You get to use the mirroring technique whenever there's a suitable opportunity. I also refer to it as the mimicking technique. It essentially requires that you pay very close attention to the body language and attributes of your prospects, and then do as they do. If they sit with their hands together, you do too. If they sit with their legs crossed, that's another cue. If they stand in a particular position, you try to mimic their stance. Even if they use a specific style or mannerism while talking or communicating, you try doing the same. Very ape, you say? Well, read on.

It's crucial that you be as discreet as possible with this technique, for if a prospect catches you imitating him/her, you'll find yourself up a creek without a paddle. Not good at all. In my years of using this technique, I have never been caught. Knock on wood, indeed.

When you use this technique, understand the "what" and "why" behind the process. What you're doing is copying the person you are in conversation with, body language, and attributes alike. Why you're doing this is to build rapport with them quickly.

From a prospect's perspective, this happens through a subconscious state of being. You basically lead your prospects' minds to think and feel that you are just like them. They gravitate to connecting with and liking you faster, to listen to you intently, and to even place their trust in you.

Do not engage in using this technique until you have completed the following exercise at least five times.

Exercise 2

A. Have a conversation with someone.
B. While doing so, pay close attention to his/her body language.
C. Notice what you see and get ready to slowly do what the other person does.
D. Copy one thing that he/she is doing or the way he/she is speaking.
E. Keep going with that one thing for a few moments.
F. Once you feel comfortable and your heart stops racing, move to do two such things.
G. Stay in the moment for a while and keep the conversation going.
H. Wrap up by letting the person know that you like him/her and that you feel good about being a part of the conversation.

Go through all the eight steps from A to H at least five times without getting caught before you try this on any of your prospects. Going forward, practice this exercise for a minimum of five days per week. At the end of each mirroring technique exercise you complete, get into a quiet place to reflect on what the other person said and his/her attributes. Then, replay in your mind what you did to mirror his/her behavior or mannerisms.

Psychological Reciprocity

According to social psychology, the principle of psychological reciprocity is a fairly basic one. What it suggests is that there are numerous social settings and conversations in which people pay back what they receive from others. What I discovered in the early 1990s, in essence, was that when you give your prospects credit for their beliefs, feelings, emotions, and/or values, they become morally obligated to reciprocate in kind.

This is one principle I use every day. After relying on it for close to three decades, it's now embedded in my system. This, to me, is the most fun part of the first step, conversation.

When I pay complete attention to my prospects, let them know I understand them well, and then give them an example of truly understanding them, they turn right around and owe me one. When I move forward to presenting what I'm selling, they express that they completely understand why my products or services will fulfill their wants, needs, and DBM. This, in turn, effortlessly and quickly moves them to close with me.

Getting the Facts

In the first step, it's very important that you not only get to connect with your prospects, but also that you complete a fact find to learn about the product that your prospect wants to buy or sell. For example, if you're involved in the sale of a house, you need to learn about the home from the perspective of the buyer and/or seller by discovering their wants, needs, and DBM.

For instance, what does a seller want out of the sale of a property? Is it to sell quickly and move on, or is it to get a particular price that's needed to pay something off? Similarly, what does a buyer want in a new property? Is it a specific number of bedrooms and bathrooms, is it particular neighborhoods within certain school zones, or is it access to an array of amenities?

Furthermore, you need to understand the reasons behind their needs. The need is an element your prospect has, and you need to look at it as a requirement that cannot be compromised.

I often come across buyers who say they want three bedrooms with two baths. However, their need extends to just two bedrooms, because they plan to use the third as an occasional guest room or office space. When putting the wants vs. needs message across, you need to be very tactful, and not at all belittling.

I always go with something like, "So, you want three bedrooms and two baths, correct?" "Awesome, I got that." I then follow it up with, "Would you say that two bedrooms can work for you at all?" Using this tactic helps me get the facts so I don't miss any opportunities for my buyer.

What if there's a property with two bedrooms that's super large when it comes to square footage, and can be converted to add another bedroom? What if a buyer really loves a two-bedroom home I show and realizes that working from home or hosting relatives once a year does not require an additional bedroom?

The last part of this step gets your state of being in line with that of your prospects and anyone else who is part of the sales process. That is how it makes them feel once they've achieved their wants and needs from you.

Only when you discover their wants and needs and let them know you understand these aspects as well as how they'll feel once they get what they desire should you move to the second step, curiosity.

To get a complete understanding of the first step, carry out the following exercise by pairing up and role-playing with someone you know. Alternatively, stand in front of a mirror and play both parts on your own. Practice it every day, for at least five days per week. Now is the best time to start, so get up!

Exercise 3

A. Get your listener to listen to you, to like you, to trust you, and to believe in you.

B. Get the listener's authority to buy, and this is anyone who will make the decision to pull the trigger and close.

C. Get your listener to disclose what he/she wants and needs.

D. Get your listener to disclose his/her dominant buying motive (DBM).

Going Deep With a Seller

I want you to practice with me. Let's do a few exercises so we can get a feel of how to connect with a seller over the phone or in-person quickly.

Example 1

I've mentioned the importance of putting a seller at ease. How do you do that? It's time for some role-playing, so here we go.

Ring, ring, the telephone rings, and the seller answers.

Me: "Hi, may I speak with John?"

Seller: "Yes, this is he."

Me: "Hello, John, this is Paul Atkinson. I'm with XYZ Realtors and I am one of the best realtors in your marketplace. The reason I'm calling today is I noticed your property just came off the market. It got me to wonder if you still want to sell."

Seller: "Yes, I do."

Me: "Well, John, before we move forward, I noticed that your telephone number comes with a 718 area code. Isn't that New York?"

Seller: "That's right, Paul."

Me: "How about that! I used to live in Brooklyn, on Saint Marks - between Nostrand Avenue and Rogers Avenue."

**See how that works? All you need to do is relax, and find a connection.
It's there alright, you just have to look.**

Example 2

Here, I'm going to a listing appointment with a seller. Let's look at what it can be like.

I am at the front door after having rung the doorbell. John opens the door.

Me: "Hi, John. I'm Paul Atkinson with XYZ Realtors. Thank you for having me over and I'm delighted to be here."

John: "Hi Paul, come on in."

Me (a few moments after I enter): "Wow, John, the open plan is great and makes for an amazing look."

Me (soon after, because I get a whiff of what's cooking): "Are you guys cooking chicken curry or something like that?"

John: "Yeah man, you're right! We're from the islands."

Me: "What a coincidence! I'm from Jamaica too. Oh, and the chicken curry, man, it smells incredible. I cook mine by burning the curry a little at first, do you too?"

Note that it's crucial to use all your senses. Use your sight, smell, hearing, taste, and touch when you want to connect with people. If you're drinking a beverage that's similar to what your prospect is drinking, be it a cocktail, a soda, or some coffee; bring taste into your conversation. For instance, if you're both drinking liqueurs, you could say something along the lines of, "Have you ever tried amaretto? I think it tastes wonderful."

Association is one of the best ways to make a connection in the first step of the sale, and it's important that you connect very quickly.

Going Deep With a Buyer

Even if you make contact with a prospect through a referral, it doesn't mean that you skip the first step and go directly to step two. That's not how it happens. You still need to go through the sales process step by step. You have to get your prospects to like you through conversation. You need to bring curiosity and conviction to the table, and even designer clothes, should the situation demand.

Example

In this case, imagine me meeting a buyer at a coffee shop, at my office, or just about anywhere. This is a prospect referred to me by someone I know.

> Me: "Hey, Tom. How are you? It's nice to meet you. Paul Atkinson. I'm glad you're here."

> Tom: "Hi, Paul. The feeling's mutual."

> Me: "Is that a Tommy Bahama shirt you're wearing?" I laugh subtly, and then add, "I have many of these, and I quite like this one. Its color is pretty amazing."

That's how easily I make a connection. How long do you think this might take? No more than 10 or 15 seconds.

**What do you notice that can help you
connect with your prospect?
What do you see, smell, taste, hear, or physically
feel that can help you establish common ground?**

No matter whether you wish to connect with a seller or a buyer, you must keep practicing. During the first step, you have to use your skills, which include association skills, mirror technique skills, and the use of psychological reciprocity.

When you make a connection, pour some love into your heart and relax. Remember that you're connected with just another human being. Even if in pretense, tell yourself, "Oh, I love them already." If you're nervous, tell yourself, "I love this prospect, and he/she is just like my brother/ sister." Stay calm, for there's no reason to be afraid. I assure you it's all going to be okay.

Persuasion and Influence

You need to know three points about persuasion and influence to continue through The Five Steps of the Sale. To become a masterful salesperson, you must realize that communication equals wealth. Once you learn how to communicate effectively, wealth will follow. If you're already wealthy, your riches will increase. I've been doing it since 1993 with great success and so can you.

You must have these three points set in your heart, soul, and mind when you're using the five steps selling system. Read these out aloud.

1. I am responsible for sending and receiving in all my communication.
2. I am getting back what I want because I am always focused and listening.
3. I always educate and inspire when I communicate, and it leads my prospects to believe they're the ones making the buying decisions at that moment.

The *first point* indicates that you are responsible for sending and receiving in all your communication, so you need to be doubly careful. Is your tone conforming? Is it in line with your prospect's tonality? Do you present yourself in a professional way that will get your prospect to like, respect, and trust you? These are very important to move a prospect from the first to the fifth step.

According to the *second point*, you get back what you want because you're focused and listening at all times. Focus and active listening are crucial. There are numerous instances when people's brains run amok even when they're in the middle of conversations. For instance, someone's talking to you and while you're mildly acknowledging through nods and monosyllables, your mind is thinking, "This food is amazing" or "I wonder what my boss may say tomorrow."

While we make it seem like we're actually listening, our minds wander all over the place. To us, all that probably registers from the conversation is yap, yap, and yap some more. Soon enough, we're wondering what we can say next. All you need to do is relax. There's no need to try and figure out what you're going to say next. You simply have to listen to what the other person has to say. Once he/she is done talking, there's could be a pause or a question.

Here's an example to help illustrate this point better. A client goes, "Hey, Paul, I want to buy a house that's got three bedrooms and two baths. I need it to be in a great community with good neighbors because of my kids and I want them to go to the best school. If I could get a pool, that would be great. If I can get a yard and an open plan, that'd be excellent too. I'm also really concerned about crime rates in the community."

While I ponder on these requirements, I hear, "Is this something you think we can find, Paul? What do you think?" At this point, I respond, "Okay. I see what you're saying. You want in this neighborhood and with all these features." I am sending and receiving.

You basically need to paraphrase and repeat what your prospects say to let them know you were listening. Remember that they might not view this as deeply as you. However, when you're dealing with a real estate buyer or seller, nine times out of ten, this is where it's going.

You might steer the initial conversation toward New York (where you're from), eating chicken curry, drinking a cup of tea, or your kids playing on the same soccer team. However, you have to listen and know that you're responsible for sending and receiving information. Consequently, you have to listen all the time. If you ever get caught not listening, it will break the trust that you work hard to build. Stay focused!

The *third point* highlights the need to always educate and inspire when you communicate. This way, your prospect feels that he/she is making the eventual buying/selling decision. Just what do you think when I say you're always educating and inspiring?

Here's an example. This time, it's me speaking with the same client. "Okay, John, so you wanted three bedrooms and two baths in a great community, correct? Well, this is an amazing home, with school ratings above your expectations. It has all the community amenities you want and more. You'll know just what I'm talking about once we step inside."

I proceed to add further details by saying, "It has the open plan you want, much to your liking. A fenced backyard will keep your kids safe. There's a pool too, which you both wanted. The home also has a two-car garage, which is perfect, given that you and your wife have separate cars. Plus, I know this is one of the top homes you'd like to see, and you're going to feel great when you get inside. Come on then, let's go take a look."

As you enter the home, make sure you say, "Welcome home." This immediately puts the buyer in a positive frame of mind. Notice here that I'm educating. I'm also inspiring. John, my buyer, can't wait to see and tour the home. This is amazing stuff.

Do not leave the first step of the sale until you complete getting all that you need. You have to get your prospects to listen to you, like you, and trust you. You also need to carry out a complete fact find. What do they want and need, and what's their DBM? As we do all that's been discussed so far, we are preprogramming the other person, the prospect.

I'm taking them, in advance, to where they want to go, and then they're going to stick with me. That's how this will lead us into Step 2, which is curiosity.

Step 2 - Curiosity

IN THE CURIOSITY STEP OF THE SALE YOU GET YOUR prospects, buyers or sellers, to a stage where they are eager hear your proposal. They become so intrigued, excited, and ready that they pay full attention to you during your presentation. This is where you get your prospect to be hungry to hear, see, smell, and even taste your proposal, if so needed.

To be hungry to see your proposal is exactly where you want your prospect to be. This allows you to take your prospect one step closer to being eager to close with you.

How do you get your prospects to want to see your proposals, for them to want to hear what you have to say? How do you get them to do that? How do you create that curiosity? It's easy, and it's breathtaking to see them in this state of complete attention.

Do you remember the first step – conversation? Did you get your prospects to like you? Did you get them to listen to you? Did you find out what they want, what they need, and what their DBM was? Did you do that? If you did, move them into curiosity. It's as easy as opening the curtains to a Broadway show. You follow this up with an amazing presentation about what you're offering to them.

How curiosity works is simple. You precisely restate what they want, what they need, and what their DBM is, and you use this information as a bridge to roll right into your presentation.

It goes a little something like this.

> Me: "Okay, Susie, you mentioned you wanted a three-bedroom two-bath home in a very good community for your kids. The school must be really good, and you wanted a home that had an open plan, a pool, and a fence, is that right?"

> Susie: "Yes."

> Me: "Susie, you also mentioned that you needed two bedrooms or more as long as it's spacious, but three-bedroom would be better. Is that correct?"

> Suzie: "Yes, Paul, that's right."

> Me: "Okay, wonderful. I have some great options for you because I know you said that once we find something like this you're going to feel very happy. I have some great opportunities because I know just how to find them. Here's what I'm going to do. I'll send you an email with at least 10 homes. Look at them, identify

the ones you like the most, and just let
me know."

You can see curiosity at work here because your buyer is now thinking, "Oh, my goodness, I really can't wait to see this list of homes." What you've basically done is restate what they want and tell them what they're going to see. Sure, it sounds simple. However, you're preprogramming the sale that's going to take place. You're getting them ready so when they see the homes that they want and need, they will be ready to sign the contract and move forward to closing.

There are different ways to present these things. Some people, or let's just say some realtors, may say, "Okay. I'm going to pick out 10 homes for you. You're going to meet me down the street tomorrow at 5 o'clock and I'll show you these homes." Some other realtor might say, "I'm going to give you a list of homes, and I'd like you to look them through. I'll call you back later so we can sit down and go over them." Some others might even say. "Hey, come into the office. Let's sit down together and I'll show you a few homes." It's common for real estate agents to use systems they are comfortable with, and it doesn't matter as long as it's done right.

Whatever you choose, it's all good. However, you always need to execute the curiosity step in a way that gets you to restate a prospect's want, need, and DBM. Remember that.

Once you're done restating, you need to get your prospect's confirmation. You need to get a confirmation on each point, and you wait for it every time. That's right; you wait for a "yes" on each point. Having said three or more yeses, you already have your prospects going, "Yes, yes, yes." Preprogramming really works, making one the "yes" guy or girl.

This is really deep. Once you pass this stage, you want to tell your prospects you have what they're looking for. So, you're going to restate their wants, needs, and DBMs. Next, you're going to get them to say, "Yes, that's what I want. Yes, that's what I need. Yes, that's how I said I'm going to feel." Then, you're going to say, "Oh my goodness, yes, I got it. You know what? I really have some great ideas. I cannot wait to show you this. Wait until we get there, I'm going to show you just what you need to see."

Here, you've got to be all fired up. You must put some enthusiasm into the process, a lot, actually. If you're in front of your prospects, I want you to use your body language. Picture yourself saying:

- "Oh, my goodness. Yes. You know what? I just showed another buyer the same type of home you're after. I know the ideal community for you. I know exactly what will make you happy, for sure."
- "Wow! I have a really good house that I want you to see. Wait till you see it, and I already think you'll love it."

In both these scenarios, your body language needs to be positive and vibrant. You need to display high energy levels during your interactions. You need to be all fired up.

Bear in mind that your body language shows through even on the phone. When you're saying something like, "Wow, Susie, I can't wait to show you this place. I'm so excited." it's important for you to be actually excited. Say the name of your prospects out once in a while. Say you can't wait to get together so you can show them the homes they seek. Then, politely end the conversation.

Here's how it can flow. "Now, we said we're going to get together and I'll show you properties at 3 o'clock on Saturday. Is that right?" "Okay great. See you then." Staying fired up with enthusiasm and maintaining high levels of performance are very important for the curiosity step of the sale.

Curiosity is where you get the prospect hungry to hear your proposal. As practical as it may sound, it's exactly what you do. Always make the prospect eager to hear your proposal.

Think about this along with the first step - conversation. Imagine a great conversation. You feel comfortable. Your heart is comfortable. You're not stressed out. Your palms are not sweating because you're cool. You're cool as a cucumber. You practice all the time.

Remember the tools I told you about in step one? You must practice, practice, and practice some more. When you practice, what you get are rewards in the form of closings. You're going to feel more comfortable.

This is a great exercise for curiosity, and it will help you make your prospects hungry to hear your proposals.

Exercise 4

1. Restate your prospects' wants, needs, and DBMs.
2. Get them to go "yes, yes, and yes."
3. Tell them you know what they want and need, and how it will make them feel.
4. Get fired up and raise your energy to the highest possible level.
5. Tell them you're very excited, and that you cannot wait to show them what they want and need, while stating their DBM again.
6. Lead them right into the next step of the sale – conviction.

Step 3 - Conviction

The third step is conviction. This is where you convince a buyer/seller to close with you right away. You make your presentation during this step, making it one of the most vital parts of The Five Steps of the Sale. It's the heartbeat of the sales process because this is where you give your impeccable presentation.

Let's get deep into the world of conviction. Does it sound a little like convict? Well, here conviction relates to your ability to convince your prospects, through your own convictions or beliefs. I want you to lay out your conviction for your prospect. This is where you need good selling skills. Not to worry, because it's all part of the process and you've already been building rapport and trust, getting connected, getting them to like you, and creating curiosity.

Once you move to the conviction stage of the sale, you'll give your prospects three main elements. These elements will lead your prospects smoothly into your presentation, fully focused and ready to make their decisions.

The first element is *preprogramming*. Remember that you started this in the curiosity step of the sale, where you preprogram a prospect's mind into signing your listing agreement or contract. You told your prospects that you have what they want and need.

If you're talking to a seller over the phone before a physical listing appointment, be sure to get all the details he/she wants you to, and this will help get the job done. This is how prospects get preprogrammed in their minds. Ensure that the information you gather can help you show them that you are the agent of choice.

During your calls, let them know that you will mail or email them information that might be of value to them or details of a pre-listing package. It is information that gives you insight into what sellers are interested in seeing in agents who list their properties. I pay close attention to and focus on what I pick up during our conversations. Asking powerful questions such as the ones that follow will go a long way in getting the seller to open up to you:

List of powerful questions to ask a seller

1. Why do you wish to sell at this point in time?
2. What was the reason your property did not sell when it was listed last (if it was listed in the past)?
3. What do you want to see in your realtor?
4. What are some of the things you need to see happen from your realtor?
5. Where would you like to go once you sell this property?

Providing sellers a pre-listing package gives them information about what it will take to list and sell a property. It also gives them an indication of what it will be like to work with you and how much you charge as fees.

Here is a list of things you may use in a pre-listing package:

1. Your resume or biography.
2. Reviews or testimonials from your previous clients.
3. Information about your brokerage firm.
4. A marketing plan with your ideas to sell their property.
5. A list of your brokerage affiliations and syndication platforms to maximize exposure.
6. Examples of your marketing materials - digital and print - are a plus.
7. Market trends and statistics from the seller's community.
8. A list of questions all sellers should ask their realtors before listing.
9. Short introductions to your transaction management, title, escrow, and closing process.
10. A pre-filled listing agreement (without the seller's listing price or your fees)

Think of anything else that will differentiate you from other agents and help sellers prepare to market their properties effectively. Personalize the package for each seller you meet. This is a great way to get their attention and show them that you are a true partner in listing with them.

The end result here is that the seller says something along the lines of, "I'm going to get all of this? Look at this package and the fancy stuff." This is preprogramming at its best.

Here is an example of what a conversation should be like when you talk to a prospect over the phone. "Hello, Mr. ABC, when I come to see you and the property, I'm going to bring a lot of information for you, and it's going to give you all that you want and need."

Sitting With the Seller

During the conviction step, when you're giving your presentation at the dining room table, preferably, you are essentially preprogramming your prospects and moving them to close. By this time, you've already found out what they want and need, and what their DBM is. Use verbal bridges that say, "I understand what you want to do by selling this home and moving to another area, either to upgrade or downgrade." State their motivation to sell.

Here's an example of what the conversation and setting should be like. Imagine sitting down at the table with a seller. One thing I must tell you about when you're doing a listing presentation with a seller – you have to get cozy, get comfortable.

What I typically do is sit on a couch, if available, and use my laptop. If that's not an option, I get print-outs of my presentation. However, I usually have my laptop and strongly recommend that you use yours.

I then say to the sellers, "Well, I have this amazing presentation I'd like to show to you. It's about just how we're going to sell your home. Would you like us to sit at the dining room table? As a matter of fact, I think it's the best place for all of us to sit for the presentation. Do you mind if one of you sits on my left and the other on the right, with me in the middle?" They typically say, "Okay, Paul. Sure!" I like to be in the middle. It's a great way to get cozy.

Bear in mind that when you do this for the first time, there's a good chance you'll be nervous. Your hands could be sweaty, and you might be like, "Oh my goodness! What's happening?" Make sure you focus on your breathing and relax, so you can get through it comfortably. After the first time, the second time, and then the third, you become very comfortable. You're like, "I just love being the middle. I got Suzie over here and Johnny over there. Yeah, we're having a drink together."

So there, make sure you have your laptop. I've got four eyes on my laptop to go with two of my own.

Start with, "What is it that you want out of this property? Why are you selling?" These are powerful questions. "What is the motivation for you to sell right now?" Your seller might say, "Well, we need to get a bigger home because we've got little Johnny running around and this space seems inadequate. We bought this house a couple of years ago. Now, there's not enough space for us all to be comfortable." You get the motivation, of which you make a mental note, because you will need it later in the sales process, should any objections arise.

Alternatively, your seller might say, "we need to move to another city because Johnny's mother lives there and we're expecting our second child." It could be practically any reason. You just find out their motivation to sell. For instance, do they need to relocate because of a job offer or transfer? You must find out what will drive them to sign the contract when they begin to pour information your way. "What's their motivation?" Ask yourself that.

"Okay, great. I understand that. You want to sell because ..." I restate the reason. Remember, you have to restate that. The next question is, "I understand your requirements correctly, right?"

If you have to say something about a prospect's needs, what would you say? "What do you need out of the real estate agent that you want to work with?" "What do you need?" I always ask this question, and they often say, "I just need to sell the house."

At this point, I ask, "I understand there are many realtors out there, but what do you think you'd like to see? Think about it - what do you want to see in your realtor?" I loosen them up a bit and they soon start to tell me everything. "Well, my friend told me that his/her realtor never came and opened up the house, and did this or did not do that." Get all the dirt you can. Do you see what's happening? It's interesting, right? It's all about wants and needs.

Once you know what your prospects want, you ask them, "What do you need?" This way, we guide them in the general direction of disclosing information. What do they want to do? What do they want to see in the realtor that they're going to work with?

Then, you go, "Okay, let me ask you a question. What would it be like when you sell your property at your desired price and based on other conditions, and then move to exactly where you want to because of an ideal realtor like me? Well, isn't that why I'm here?" Be sure to laugh slightly when you say this, and don't go over the top.

Continue with. "How would it make you feel once you achieve all this?" How I feel the seller usually replies is, "We're going to feel amazing, man. We're going to feel good." You then say, "Excellent! Well, I'm going to show you just how we're going to do that."

You then carry forward with your presentation. Here's an example of how it can flow. "Let's look at my screen. Here's what I want to show you. This is the market condition right now. These are the active listings, these are pending sales, and these are the sold properties. They all make up the market that you're going to enter. As you can see, we have 15 active properties at this moment, and we have around 10 that are pending sale or back up, which essentially means they're going to close out real soon."

You continue, "Note that this a good advantage, because if something is close to the number you're after, we'll talk to individuals in question. I'll check and see if they're going to get their desired price, or will it be more or less? If they are getting their asking price or above, it's going to help you get your price as well."

Then, you say something like this. "This is the technique I'm using for you. Now, let's look at the closed sales. This is where appraisals matter. No matter what price tag we put on your property, it needs to pass appraisal in order to close. We want to make sure we don't overprice the property, unless you don't mind being on the market for a long time as opposed to selling quickly. Whatever you prefer, though, it's perfectly okay by me."

Next, you move to talk about price. Use a verbal bridge like this. "Now, John, Susie, how much money were you thinking about getting for your property? What is your idea of pricing?"

Let's say the seller replies, "Oh, well, we were thinking about $450,000." You say, "Okay. So, let's take a look at the market right now," and proceed to show them the current market. You add, "John and Susie, do you see these right here? These are the active listings. There's one for $700,000 and there's another for like $300,000, and then, there are a few in the middle."

Show all that you see and compare their property to the others. Then ask, "Where do you want to be in the marketplace because these are your competition?" Your seller may say something like, "Well, we were thinking about coming out at $450,000, but that's going to put us so high. Maybe we do $425,000. What do you think, Paul?"

That's how I work. Now, other people may do it differently but in the five steps of the sales program, this is how I partner with my sellers. I get them to jointly work with me and then close the listing right there on the spot.

When we partner up, we arrive at the price that our prospects want to see and are comfortable with, although it may take a different direction in some cases. For example, there's an instance of overpricing where the seller says, "You know, Paul, I don't care what the market says. I want $500,000. I know that the last sale comparable was $450,000 but maybe somebody will pay."

Should this happen, remember that it's perfectly okay. Just go for it. Tell your prospects you understand how they feel, and that you're there to support them. Say something like, "I'm your realtor. It's going to be fine. But let's set up a price reduction format from here." What you also tell them is, "Okay, we're going to start $500,000."

"We'll start there, let's write this down." Then, say, "If we don't get any showings in three weeks, this is what the scenario might look like." You basically paint the picture for your seller. You add, "The first drop in price could be $5,000 or $7,000 - which do you feel is better?" The reply is, "I guess $5,000 should be okay". You then say, "All right. Great! What's the next drop? Do you feel good at

$5,000 again or $3,000?" The seller's reply is, "Yes, $5,000 should work." From here, lead the seller to the close.

See how this trial closing works. "John and Suzie, I feel so happy to know that you trust me as you realtor and that we've now put together a plan to sell this property. Here is our listing agreement, let's complete it together."

That's how you do it. The conviction step of the sale is very critical. The most important aspects include making sure you have already connected with your prospects, and ensuring that you're going to show them what they want and need, and what their DBM is.

That's the most important part. Bear in mind that you're going to use the preprogramming skills you have developed or are developing as well as your body language. Remember the undeniable truth, because should you need it, you must use it.

The Undeniable Truth

The undeniable truth is where you make three points based on your prospects' desires. For example, if you're going to use the undeniable truth for your seller, it's something like this. "Suzy and John, you want to sell to move closer to your mom, correct? In this presentation, I've given you the latest information about the market condition, I've shown you all the marketing tools I'm going to use, and I've highlighted how we are going to respond to offers."

Follow it up with, "You want an agent who's going to be there at open houses and be there for you. How do you feel about that right now? Does this satisfy everything that you're looking for?" The seller says, "Yes, Paul." You go, "Wonderful! We're going to start at $500,000, is that right?" The seller says, "Yes, that's correct." Write that down and then say, "Let's go over this agreement together and set our first open house."

You have to be strong all through the sales process and stay with positive thoughts Make sure you use the trial closing along each and every step of the way. Don't forget, you must practice, practice, and practice some more.

Talking With the Buyer

When you're talking with a buyer during the conviction step of the sale, work at achieving the preprogramming principles already described. For example, let it be along the lines of, "Carl, I have found your new home and you're going to love it." That's preprogramming. Alternatively, you may say, "Hey, Carl, I found the perfect home for you and I'm sure you'll love it" or "Carl, you wanted wooden floors, an updated kitchen, and an open plan, and that's just what I found."

Let's go through what this should look like with prospective buyers. They're following you in their car. It's Carl and Mary. You pull up to the property and use a verbal bridge like, "Okay guys, yeah, this is the one. I remember this one well. It has a backyard and everything else you want."

This is what you remember and know because you did your rehearsal by forming pictures that matched their wants and needs, right? You may have even visited the property before you pull up with your clients and walk them through it, so you already have a visual of that. Make sure you get out of your car all fired up – brimming with enthusiasm and the desire to educate – and energized to the core.

Even before you enter, say, "All right, Mary, Carl, let me tell you something right now. This house has three bedrooms and two baths. It has the open plan, the updated kitchen, and the fenced backyard you want. I can't wait to show it to you. Come on, let's take a look, guys." Bam! You're preprogramming again.

When I open a door for my buyers, I like to say, "Step in, guys. Welcome home." Yeah, I like to do that a lot. In fact, I do it all the time, with pretty much all the houses I show, I know beyond a shadow of doubt that the homes fit my buyers to the T. That's why I say, "Welcome home" at every showing. If I show five houses, I say "welcome home" five times, and buyers usually start to laugh light-heartedly. That's the technique I use, and it works rather well.

As we get close to finishing seeing a home, right at the end, I say, "So, Carl and Mary, what are you guys feeling right now?" or "What are you both feeling about this home right now?" I do this because I'm preprogramming them to close.

"What do you feel?" That's what you ask as you're about to wrap it up, just before your prospects are about to leave. Do this in an environment in which you feel comfortable. Think about it closely.

Don't do this outside under the hot sun where everybody's sweating. Your prospects probably won't even be able to think straight because of the heat. If a woman's a part of the deal, she surely won't want her makeup running. I know this because I've been there many times. This also holds true for when the weather is cold as well.

Ideally, keep them indoors and find a good spot. Make sure there's adequate circulation of air because you might end up sweating. This is natural. I still sweat at times, even after over 25 years of doing what I do best. You might be a little apprehensive or scared when going through this process for the first time. However, after a while, when you've practiced your way to perfection, you'll notice that you're absolutely calm each and every time.

Once you have your buyers in a comfortable spot, use a verbal bridge to move them to a close and write the offer. Asking "What do you guys feel about this house?" or "What are you guys feeling?" works well.

When buyers reply positively and inch toward making an offer, they may say something like, "Oh, you know, Paul, yeah, this is good. It has everything that we want. We really like it a lot, so we want to move forward. I mean, this is good." At this stage, you should reply energetically and say something like, "I knew you would like it." Then, go for a trial close by using a verbal bridge like, "What do you think you'd like to offer?"

This process is smooth. It's like a glove that comes with the perfect fit. You're not being pushy or demanding, so they don't feel pressure. Often, they feel like you're a well-meaning brother or sister who's guiding them in the right direction. Can you imagine that?

Here's an example of the conviction step when dealing with buyers.

You're showing a home to a couple. You get them in there and highlight all the features and benefits. Right toward the end, you bring them to a comfortable spot. If you can't do this for some reason such as the seller or a listing agent also being home at the same time, that's okay too.

In such a scenario, you could say, "Okay, guys, I can see you want to talk on this one," or "I know it's hot/cold," "so would you be okay with doing the talking while driving around for a bit?" Be safe here and choose when you wish to have the conversation. Then, don't forget to have the conversation.

Here's another scenario that may occur with your buyer, where you have to drive to the next showing. If you're all in the car together, make sure you're driving because you need your buyers' complete attention.

What you say during this conversation should be along the lines of this example.

"So, guys, we're headed to the next home on the list now. However, what do you feel about the one we just saw?" Always say "feel." Remember their DBM and that they're going to feel happy. You have already preprogrammed them from way back in the first step, conversation. You're basically making use of the roots of what you've built. Once you ask them, "Hey, what do you guys feel about the house we just saw?" stop talking and take a deep breath. Let them do the talking now.

Let them think about what they feel. This is when you might expect a moment or more of silence. This is a natural state, and you need to give them time to process their thoughts.

Then, you're going to hear what the husband or the wife has to say. When this is happening, stay calm. After all, they're just going to talk. You'll know when they want to make an offer, and you can then move into the conversation and go for that trial close.

Remember that you always want to know when you can move to the trial close. It is part of a secret to closing that you must have in your arsenal at all times. It's like dropping breadcrumbs along the way during your sales process, and it tells you when a close is about to happen. You need to look for and try it all the time.

A trial close is nothing more than you saying, "Okay, what are you feeling?" Consider this example. "Carl, and Mary, what do you feel about this beautiful home here?" When one of them says, "This is great. I really can see our furniture fitting in it. Right honey?" they're confirming with each other. That's when you know you need to pull the trigger and close.

When you hear your buyers say things like "the furniture would fit", "everything looks good," "the schools are great," or "Little Carl will love this place," know that these are indications that they are ready to close and write an offer. Listen carefully and pay attention to details.

What do you do at this point to close the sale? You simply say, "Oh, wow! I feel the same way. I knew you guys would like this house. How much do you think you'd like to offer?" This is a trial close – simple yet effective.

A buyer may proceed by asking, "How much is the seller expecting to get?" You mention the asking price - let's say $450,000 - and add something along the lines of, "I've looked at comparable sales. Given that I know this area well, I already have a good feeling about the comparables. The highest sale amount in the last six months is $475,000, with all upgrades. Since this is a really tough market, I recommend you make an offer of $450,000 or $460,000. This is because you'll need to carry out some upgrades."

Alternatively, I may say, "I've looked at comparable sales, and the value of the house is between $430,000 and $450,000. However, the home needs an upgrade. I would estimate paying around $20,000 for the kitchen's makeover. I think we could try at $430,000 and work our way up so we don't lose the deal. What do you both feel?"

No matter what, always give your professional advice. However, the most important thing to remember during this stage is to carry out the trial close and move your prospects forward. I love how this works.

Excited much? Well, you should be because I've been doing this day in and day out since 1993, and it's produced great results.

Interesting, isn't it? You need to use your body language and all the other techniques discussed so far. Remember the undeniable truth, where you need to make three points based on your prospects' desires. You use this technique when a buyer seems hesitant to say yes and make an offer.

The Undeniable Truth

This, again, is where you give units of conviction. Keep in mind that three units make for a solid conviction. Every unit of conviction helps you to present your proposal in a way that gets prospective buyers to justify buying on the spot. They justify it because you've put itsy-bitsy pieces together to present an entirety of evidence to them till you reach a stage where they are ready to close with you.

This is when you have all the evidence of closing through what they want, what they need, and how they are going to feel amazing. This, in essence, includes their wants, needs, and DBM. For example, you say, "Carl, as you walk through this home, you see the open plan, the updated kitchen, and the wooden floor you truly desire in your new home."

The Undeniable Truth
*Use three true points based on what
your prospects Want or Need.*

You must keep a positive mindset all through the conviction process. Use the Nuclear Mind technique to have the right mindset with every buyer. No matter what happens, remember these words:

1. Control
2. What
3. You
4. Can
5. Control

Then, move your buyer to write a strong offer. Practice, practice, and practice some more.

Step 4 - Desire

THE FOURTH STEP IS DESIRE, AND IT'S TYPICALLY NOT needed. This is because when you go through steps one, two, and three impeccably, you bypass step four and get right to the fifth, which is close. In reality, this step of the sale requires nothing more than objection handling.

Professional salespersons realize that their prospects have difficulty in making decisions. They recognize that prospects are challenged by "why" and "why not" and lack the psychological reciprocity needed to close. They understand that this puts their prospects on the defensive. This notwithstanding, your prospect may react negatively at a trial close for one or more of the following reasons:

A. The prospect needs more information to make a decision.
B. The prospect is testing your conviction.
C. The prospect is trying to keep from making a decision.
D. The prospect has a real and possibly hidden concern.

As a top salesperson, you need to know that you must not attempt to handle an objection until you know what's on your prospect's mind.

A number of sales are lost for this very reason. At this stage, you must be careful with your choice of words in order to handle objections effectively. For example, you do a trial close with a buyer or seller, saying, "How do you feel about this home?" to a buyer, or "Are you ready to do an open house this weekend?" to a seller. Only, you get a negative response. Your verbal bridge should then be something like, "You obviously have a reason for saying that, John, do you mind if I ask what it is?"

This response should be so conditioned into your mind that it becomes automatic. Note the difference in the "You obviously …" vs. "Why not?" when you get a no.

With this technique, I always find that my buyers and sellers give me their conditions to move forward with me. This is what you want to achieve. You need to understand what will make them feel comfortable to close the deal straightaway.

Keep in mind that all real objections are just questions in disguise. You must practice turning the objections you encounter into questions by using suitable lead-in bridges, much like the "You obviously …" verbal bridge we just used. When you practice, think of this. Remove the sting out of the words you choose to ensure you do not put your prospect on the defensive. I have seen it all the time. Be careful and study this technique well.

Even though you don't really need this step if you get the first three right, it's best to go through it, for you never know when it might help.

What is desire? By now your brain is probably like, "What in the world is Paul talking about?" If you're worried or feel that there's been an overload of information, remember that as long as you keep going over this system time and time again, you'll get a hang of it and you will be fine.

Even though I've been at it since 1993, I'm still practicing. Why am I still practicing? For one, I'm now learning how to sell to millennials. As we grow older, a lot changes. You will find that making a connection with people today is not the same as it was many years ago. However, these techniques are still highly effective, and you can use them to great effect even in tomorrow's world.

As time changes, you need to keep adapting and practicing, while hanging on to the same basic principles of The Five Steps of the Sale. Think of it as martial arts. A kick is still a kick and a punch is still a punch. They hurt. Keep practicing and you will defeat your opponent.

Reflect on what you have discovered through this book until now. You've read about conversation, curiosity, and conviction.

Getting back to "What is desire and what's it all about?" Well, as I just said, we don't really need the desire step of the sale. We're supposed to go from step one that includes great conversation, making connections, and fact-finding, to step two where we make our prospects hungry to receive our proposal. This is when their mind is telling them, "I can't wait to see this property. I can't wait to get the buyers in here and sell my property."

You then move to step three and show them how it's going to go down for them after they get all they want and need. When you're in this part of the conviction step, you simply skip desire. You don't need this step because you have already gotten your prospects to like you, trust you, and believe in you. This, in turn, fans their desire to close with you and only you.

When you skip the fourth step, your prospects go to close all on their own, telling you they want your product. Amazing, isn't it?

In any case, let's take a close look at desire and so you're ready to handle objections effectively. Consider this scenario. You go through the process of building rapport as well as through the curiosity stage by giving your presentation, only to have your buyer or seller say something like, "Let me think about it, we have to meet with other realtors" or "I don't want to make an offer right now."

The truth is I have been through such instances a number of times. I've sat there with prospects, I've shown them everything, I've confirmed their wants, needs, and DBM, and I've gone with a verbal bridge like, "Okay, let's get started today." Then, I get a lackluster, "No, let's think about it," or "Oh, no, we have to interview two more agents," or "Oh, I'm not prepared to make an offer yet."

This is where you need to use the fourth step – desire. In essence, this is nothing more than objection handling in its rawest form. When your client or prospect is not ready to wrap up the deal and sign the contract, you get in there and use the desire technique.

Creating desire involves attempting to disturb your prospects emotionally. You want them to dig deep into their emotions. We do this using bridge words and language that appeal to their senses and emotions. This language is referred to as concrete language. You paint a word picture that mentally puts your prospect at a specific point in time enjoying his/her DBM.

We can handle objections fairly easily by saying something along the lines of, "Susie, you said you wanted three bedrooms and two baths with an open plan, and that would make you feel happy? Is that still the same or did anything change?" If it's with a seller, you could say something like, "John, you want to sell and move closer to your mom so she can help with your new baby, and everyone would then feel at peace, correct? Is there anything we missed?"

Using Desire with a Buyer

Here's an example. I say, "I know we've seen three houses until now and nothing seems to have caught your attention to move forward. What are you feeling right now?" That's how you get into desire. With this question, you're still looking for that trial close to say, "Hey, how much would you like to offer to the seller?"

The fact is that at this juncture, should you get there, noticing that you won't have a chance to say, "Let's make the offer today," you need to realize that it's still ok to be involved. At this stage, you must make sure you confirm what your clients want and if there's anything that's standing in their way.

Here, you have to move past any objection by restating their wants, needs, and DBM. As in the recent example, use a verbal bridge with the buyer and ask, "Do you still want the same thing and need the same thing, and would you still feel the same way when you find them?"

This works in creating desire in a buyer, which, in turn, leads you to a close. The verbal bridge you use to restate their desires brings out their objections. When you do this, you typically find your prospects saying things like, "Well, yes. But I don't know if my brother, my sister, or my boyfriend … …," or whatever. Suddenly, something comes up. You may even hear, "I don't know if my fiancé is going to like this?" Up to this point, you've never heard of a fiancé and you're suddenly in a state of shock.

Not to worry, because here's the way forward. You say to the buyer, "That's okay." Put them at ease. Then, continue by saying, "We could deal with that. I remember when we spoke earlier and I asked you if there was anyone else that needed to be a part of your buying process. Do you recall us speaking about that?" Then, quickly add, "This has happened before and there's no need to worry. I know just how to get your fiancé all that she needs to feel amazing about you buying your home today."

At this stage, you'll find that you're still processing the conversation step of the sale. What? Feel like you're going backward? Where you should have asked them, "Who will help you make a decision?" or perhaps, "When you're making the decision to buy your house, is there anyone else who needs to be a part of the process?" Even though you know you've completed this stage, the buyer brings another person into bed, and the equation changes.

Let's go even further. Sometimes, prospects might say, "It's just me." While you're getting deep into the process, they flip the script on you. Just know that it's okay. You simply have to learn how to deal with such situations. The best thing you can do is use desire and make sure you're headed in the right direction, toward closing. So, yes, it's okay.

Handle the objection in this case by involving the other person in your sales process. I see this fairly often. As a matter of fact, it is very often. Unfortunately, many realtors and salespeople don't know how to recover when this happens.

What to do when in such a scenario? Be smooth and let your buyer know it's perfectly okay. Say, "With due respect to your new advisor, please invite him/her to the process."

Get your prospects together with those blocking your sale and include them in the process.

What changes here is you'll need to go through the first three steps again, to get both the buyer and the advisor to close with you and write that contact. This is how you can ensure that they're on the same page. Once you get past this, get back to the third step, conviction. Lay out an amazing presentation so all your buyers are ready to pull the trigger and sign the contract.

I want you to understand something very basic in nature. The desire step is not used often, especially if you've done a superb job with steps one, two, and three. That's conversation, curiosity, and conviction. Once you've gone through these masterfully, you may well forget about desire because your prospects go straight to close.

Get this – with 95% of the people I'm selling something to, that's exactly the route we take. It goes step one, step two, step three, and then bam, we close.

Close. It's great, no doubt, but it takes time. You must develop these skills with practice and you must give it your best. You must work your way through every step. Study each step closely and in detail. This is not something you just blow over. You need to study, work on, and practice each step.

Moving on, what about objections a seller might have?

Using Desire With a Seller

You discovered your sellers' DBM and gave a professional and well-organized presentation by maintaining the law of psychological reciprocity. Then, you're there, sitting at the dining room table with your sellers. You're in the middle, they're right next to you, and it's all warm and fuzzy.

After your presentation, you get ready for the trial close and say something like, "Okay, guys. So, how do you feel? Do you feel good about moving forward and launching your marketing plan? We can put the property on the market, and I could do an open house next weekend."

You can also say, "Well, Suzy and John, we can start by next weekend through an open house. Do you have time? We could do something like 12:00 pm to 3:00 pm. Does that sound okay?" That's another trial close. When they say, "Yes," you say, "Let's sign the forms to get you started."

However, what do you do should if Suzy and John say no? What if, after your trial close, both look at you and say, "We don't want to move that fast. We have to interview some more realtors."

How do you respond to that? It's heartbreaking. I've been there. Relax, calm down. All you have to do is just handle the objection. Sure, some of the objections you need to handle in this step might seem more challenging than the ones mentioned here. Rest assured, Exercise 5 gives you plenty to go with when handling any objection that may come your way through a seller or a buyer.

For now, I'm going to highlight one objection and show you how I would handle it. Imagine a seller objecting to signing by saying something like, "Paul, we like what you have to offer but we have to meet other realtors." My reply is, "Oh, gosh! Suzy, John, you're going to interview more realtors today? I thought you guys like me, for real. I'm sitting here busting my chops, and you don't even like me? Come on!"

At times, they even hit me on the shoulder, saying, "Paul, no, no! Don't feel like that. It's not at all like that, Paul!" Then, I say, "I'm just kidding guys. You obviously have a reason for saying that John. Do you mind if I ask what it is? Listen, I hear this often, but tell me, what do you feel, Suzy and John, that the other realtors are going to show you that I'm not showing you? Let's just take a look. Did you say you like me?" They say, "Yes." I add, "Do you trust me?"

At this point, I'm ready to hear something like, "Yeah, I mean, you're a really nice guy. Yeah, we saw you online, Paul, and you have good reviews." Then, I ask, "Okay, so what do you think the other realtors will have that I don't have?"

The seller may say, "Well, my mom always told me to check all my options." A great reply to this would be, "Listen, John, I know how you feel and other people have felt that way. However, if you feel good right now, at this moment, we can move forward. You can tell the other realtors you found who you've been looking for. What is standing in your way from doing that right now?"

Use a verbal bridge like, "Are you ready to get the price you truly want to see? We can do the open house next week and get your property under contract with the right buyer." When you get that "Yes," go over the listing agreement and get your prospects to sign. Thank them for trusting and believing in you, and let them know you are with them all the way.

Great salespeople know that prospects' objections are just a way of saying that they are not significantly disturbed by their problems. When a prospect objects to signing your contract or agreement to move forward, this prospective buyer or seller is not aware of the problem that exists in needing to take side with your proposal. In their minds, they're thinking it's not a big deal and that it's okay if they wait for more information or options.

Keep this in mind and approach this step of the sale in the right manner if you hope to become a masterful salesperson. Know that you will need to disturb such clients' beliefs and thoughts. Do this and you will easily overcome most of the objections that come your way.

All you have to say to yourself when you hear the first objection from a client is, "This client is not significantly disturbed by his/her problem and I am going to change that now."

Here are some common objections buyers and sellers may throw your way along with a few techniques on how to become a master objection handler. Keep in mind that the best way to handle objections is by practicing handling them in your own mind. This requires that you carry out role-playing every day.

Common Buyer and Seller Objections

1. I've never heard of you or your company.
2. I don't think I am ready yet.
3. Can you lower your commission?
4. You agent's commission is very high.
5. I am afraid I will not qualify.
6. Market prices are extremely high right now.
7. I am not getting to see any homes in my price range.
8. I will only sell it as-is and do not wish to do any work on the property.
9. I will not lower my price.
10. I want to find a home before listing this property.
11. We see you've not have sold any homes in our price range.
12. We will fix a few things first and then be ready to list.

Once you get an objection, start by repeating it to your prospect and then move into your presentation of answering their question. This includes reconfirming your prospects' wants, needs, and DBM.

For example, you can say something like, "Carl, I understand how you feel. Others have felt that way. May I ask a question?" Pause, don't rush the process, and take two to three seconds while still looking them in the eye. "Sure," your prospect says.

At this point, say "Thank you, Carl. You mentioned earlier that you wanted XYZ, is this correct? Perfect, I got that. You stated that you needed ABC, is that right? Well, I got that too. You also said that getting what you want and need will make you feel XYZ way. So, we are not missing anything here and you can see how my proposal will give you all that you want and need?" Mention their wants and needs again at this stage, and remind them how they will feel when they achieve them.

Once you go through this and you notice your prospects' body language and feedback is positive, move in with another trial close. You may say, "Wonderful, I'm happy to feel the way you feel now and know that working together is a great choice."

With a buyer, say something like, "How much do you feel we should offer?" If you're dealing with a seller, say, "We can set the first open house for this weekend. Are you available for us to get it done on Saturday or Sunday?" Then get your contract in to your new client's hands immediately and close the deal.

What happens if, even after this, your prospect does not want to move forward? Relax; you have already done an amazing job by following all my steps. Should such prospects choose not to move forward after you complete all the steps, simply ask them what is standing in their way of moving forward at that point in time (if they haven't told you already). Then, let them know you understand and respect their choice. Next, move the prospect forward by setting up your next meeting with him/her immediately.

Remember that there's no pressure, and results will come. Stick to thinking positive thoughts.

When you are role-playing multiple objections every day, like the ones on page 80 as well as others, you will develop the best answers and directions to make your presentations superb.

Going Deep With a Seller or Buyer

Let's take the first example from the "Common Buyer and Seller Objections" and use it for both, the buyer and the seller. The prospect says, "I haven't heard of you or your company."

Relax, and then say, "I understand how you feel, and I know you're not the first. However, because of the connection and trust I share with my clients, they always want to work with me and my company. Are you feeling the same right now? Do you feel comfortable working with me?" The prospect typically says, "Yes." You then add, "This is wonderful. I am so happy to know this, and I also feel rather comfortable working with you. Here is my contract/agreement, let's complete it together now."

If a prospective buyer says, "No," you say, "Oh, no! I thought you liked me, felt comfortable, and saw all that my company and I would do to get you the best possible home and deal." To a seller, you may tweak this slightly and say, "Oh, no! I thought you liked me, felt comfortable, and saw all that my company and I would do to get your home sold."

Handling Objections Effectively

To handle objections effectively, you must anticipate them and cut them off at the pass. When you give your prospects offers they can't refuse, they always close with you. Ask yourself the following questions and write down the answers. Completing this exercise will help you with objection handling.

Exercise 5

1. What does it mean to you when your prospect is not significantly disturbed by his/her problem?
2. Do you feel that an objection is just an opportunity to get past what is standing in your prospect's way of making the deal happen? Provide a detailed explanation.
3. Did you complete the first three steps of the sale in a masterful way?
4. Do you know your prospect's Want?
5. Do you know your prospect's Need?
6. Do you know your prospect's DBM?

Next, make time in your schedule to role-play all possible objections you can think of every day, for the next 30 days.

Role-playing for objection handling is the best exercise to become a master at selling and closing. When you practice every day, whether in front of the mirror or with someone, you're no longer afraid of hearing "no," and you get to a level of comfort that allows you to move your prospect forward. Be ready, because you never know what you're going to hear.

If you're part of a strong selling team, you guys could probably meet in the morning, telling each other to do a few role-play exercises. "Hey, I heard this objection, which I had to handle yesterday. Let me run it by you." That's how easy it can be.

You have to practice objection-handling, and you have to role-play a lot, preferably with others. You may even use your family members, if needed.

This is what you could say to the person with who you plan to role-play. "Hey, can you do me a favor and role-play with me. Can you be a nasty seller? Even though I give you an amazing presentation and ask you if you're ready to sign, you simply say, "No, get out of here." Yes, that's what I want you to say."

That's how it's done. You actually go through the process by practicing and giving your presentation, and then, all of a sudden, the seller or buyer says, "No."

I want you to get that "Oh, my goodness" feeling when someone says "no." Feel your heart racing and your palms sweating. Then, do it over and over again until you begin to relax, stay calm, have a clear mind, and are able to follow my techniques.

You could also practice by saying to the person helping you, "Okay, listen, I'm going to give you two options. You could say yes or no. It's your choice, and I don't know what to expect. I'm going to start by giving you my presentation. Ready? Okay, here we go." Practicing this exercise makes you comfortable to hear either a Yes or No. You then know how to react and move the prospect forward, no matter what.

Trust me, role-playing works.

Back to where we were - this is the fourth step of the sale, desire. It's not needed if you've done well in steps one, two, and three. Besides, it's nothing but objection-handling. However, you must develop your skills to handle objections effectively by practicing repeatedly. Do not take it for granted.

Now, let's move to the final step of the sale.

Step 5 - Close

HERE, WE ARE THEN, AT THE FINAL STEP OF THE SALE. This is where we want to go. You want to close a deal. You want the money, the moolah, right? Lock it up. Get that contract. Then, you can start to imagine, "Oh, I got to pay this bill, and pay it I shall. I can buy this and that. I could do this and that." Don't we all want to get there?

When you get there, don't you feel great? The final step is for you to close without any objections at all. Smooth as butter.

Now, though, let me tell you of a secret to closing. Since 1993, the secret to closing for me is being professional and knowing when to close. Yes, that's right. The secret to closing is to know when to close.

Consider this scenario. You start out in a conversation and build it very well - that's step one. Then, you made your prospect curious to hear your proposal - step two is out of the way. Next, you get to the third step, conviction, and are about to begin your presentation. Before you start, your prospect says, "Hey, you know what? I can't wait to work with you."

Right at this point, without going any further, great salespersons will close. This is because they know the secret to close is to go for it immediately after a prospect indicates that he/she is ready to buy.

Along the way of building the conversation, of creating curiosity, and of smoothening yourself into the conviction stage, you need to know that you should be able to start throwing out some trial closes and get an indication of how your prospects feel even in the first step. You see if they are ready to close.

If you're dealing with a seller in the first step, you could say, "Hey, we could be doing open houses next week." That's a trial close right at the beginning. Continue by saying, "Oh, yes. I can't wait to get this house on the market. You're going to be so excited to see all the work that we're going to do and all the buyers we're going to get for you." The seller's reply could be, "Oh, really?" to which you say, "Absolutely!" The seller could then go, "Oh, my goodness. I mean, I would be so happy if you could do that, Paul." That's a trial close that did the trick.

Trial closes are used within The Five Steps of the Sale at any time and all the time. They let you test the waters and they also help you preprogram the minds of your prospects to close with you.

In this example, you're dealing with buyers and are showing them a house. When they're walking through it, say, "How about that! Look at the open plan and the pool you said you wanted. Look at all this other stuff right here." As you're walking around, you open the blinds and say, "Oh, wow! I can't believe this house has all that you want. You love it, right?" That's a successfully carried out trial close because their reaction is, "Oh, yes. This seems perfect! Yes!"

Soon, you begin to see your buyers discussing placement of furniture, saying, "We could put the couch over there, and the TV could go here." At this point, be prepared but let them soak it all in. You just stand there like a fly on the wall, out of their way. If they look in your direction, move out of their view. Get out of their vision. Let them take it all in.

Then, when they're done looking, with you having participated in their viewing of the home and having recognized how they are feeling about it, they will respect you for your patience. This, in turn, leads you smoothly into closing.

All you have to do with your buyers is to continue carrying out trial closes. You already had a trial close by you saying, "Oh, wow! I can't believe this house has all that you want. You love it, right?" and your buyer saying, "Oh, yes, this seems perfect! Yes!" Trial closes such as this get your buyer ready to sign the contract.

Here's another trial close technique that works wonders. You finish up and your prospects are about to leave. Just then, you look them in the eyes and say, "Hang on a moment, guys. What are you feeling about this one?"

They go, "Paul, we love it. Oh my gosh. How do we get this one? We really want this house."

At this point, you become a part of their excitement and raise your energy levels, to the max. You say, "Okay. Great! I agree this is perfect for you. What do you think we should offer?" Boom! That's it, right there. You move straight to closing by getting ready to make a note of the terms they want included in the contract offer.

Let's assume this is how it goes. The buyers say, "We want to offer the full price." You reply, "Okay, good. As far as the deposit, we could put down $10,000. I think we should be good with that. Are you guys okay with that?" They say, "Sure, sounds good to us." You add, "Great. So, you have your checkbook?"

No matter what it takes, you get the check on the spot, made payable to the escrow account holder. Alternatively, you may get them to send a wire. These are actions that move your clients into closing with you at that very moment.

Here's a quick story from when I got my real estate license in 2003. I took my exam at eleven o'clock in the morning, on November 23rd. I wrapped up by around one o'clock and found out that I passed soon after. I worked as a financial planner at the time, so I headed back to my office to deal with clients.

In all honesty, I got my license just to help my brother, who did real estate mortgages for buyers. As I walked into the office, I said, "Hey, bro. I passed that real estate test." He replied, "I knew you would" and quickly added, "Hey, call this guy. He's approved for $250,000, and he's got FHA financing."

I'd only just received my license. I was like, "What!?" I got the information from my brother. I went to my desk, put the paper down, and started calling my clients. Then, I said to myself, "Okay, wait a second. Call this guy."

So, I made the call. The guy at the other end said he wanted to see houses in a place I'd never heard of before. I wrote that down and asked him, "When do you want to see the houses?" His reply was, "My wife and I are available this evening." That put me in shock for a moment, after which I asked him if around six o'clock would be alright. He said, "Yes, 6 pm is good," and I said, "Okay. No problem."

With my heart racing and me feeling a little panicky, I put everything together by the evening. From getting my license activated and registered, to selecting homes and previewing them, to bringing a blank contract with me on the showing, to closing that very night after writing my first contract and collecting the buyer's deposit, I did it all less than a day.

I realized that I closed my first deal on the very first day of getting my real estate license. Well, I had been using The Five Steps of The Sale since the 1990s and they definitely helped – right on day one. Interesting? When are you going to start?

Follow the five steps, dear reader, because they make for an amazing technique. I've used it for so long that I'm absolutely comfortable with it now. I'm here to teach it to you and I'm here to practice with you so you can become the masterful salesperson that you want to be.

Let's quickly relook at the five steps of the sale presented until now. They include Conversation, Curiosity, Conviction, Desire, and Close. You must learn each and every step. You must practice each and every step. You must develop each and every step by following the guidance provided to you.

There are full-blown videos that we have produced for you along with a number of courses and ways to master the system. Congratulations on finding The Five Steps of the Sale. Now, I want to empower you so you may achieve great heights by saying something I always do - "Let's go get em, Tiger."

Find our courses and more support
at www.paulratkinson.com

Making the Transformation

NOW THAT YOU KNOW HOW TO INSTILL A NEW SELLING system into your everyday life, what comes next? How do you make the transformation and become the best-selling person in your market?

The answer is to fall back on The Five Steps of the Sale. You need to embrace all five steps, and not just the parts you think might work well for you. Use and become a master in every step. Start by understanding that you need all the tools I've mentioned in earlier pages. Do you remember them? Here they are again:

- The Right Perception
- Dressing and Professionalism
- Ability to Gain Trust
- Ability to Read the Playing Field
- Ability to Use Association and Mirror Techniques
- The Right Mindset- The Nuclear Mind
- Positive Expectation (PE)
- Persuasion and Influence
- Practice

You need to have all the tools, concepts, techniques, and skill sets in place to master this technique. This selling system is fun, it's heartwarming, it's real, and most importantly, it will help you close 99% of your deals.

Marking the transformation might not be easy because we've usually been stuck with our habits for several years. However, change will occur only when you truly desire it deep down inside of you. I wanted in the 1990s. I wanted to make a good living. I wanted to stop feeling the pain of failure. Then, I decided to use a system. I've revealed this system for the first time, to you, my reader.

If you want this to become a part of the new you, simply put your heart to actually wanting it. See what it can do for you. Equip yourself with the required tools. Use materials that best fit your learning style and practice the five steps over and over again.

Look within yourself and discover what it will take to get rid of old habits and mindsets from your life today. Then, replace them with the new habits that come with using this selling system. Think positive all along the way. Manifest every event to reflect your positive expectations.

With all pretty much said and done, how do we measure our selling skills?

For around three decades, I have studied and grasped this concept, using it to propel myself through all aspects of sales and negotiations. No matter whether you wish to sell insurance, cars, computers, airplanes, or real estate, this technique always works. However, how do you measure your selling skills? Besides, why do you need to measure your selling skills?

You measure your selling skills through micro reflections after every time you use The Five Steps of the Sale, after every time you engage with a prospect. You reflect on your actions as well as those of your prospects. You ask yourself if you went through all the steps in the right manner and to the best of your abilities. What was amazing? What was weak? What could be improved?

This way, you work at identifying your strengths and weaknesses. Then, you improve them with each passing day.

Measuring your selling skills helps you to see your performance clearly. Just like any world-class champion, analyzing your performance gives you the opportunity to make improvements, to get better at what you do each day. This selling methodology must become a part of you. You take it with joy, knowing that it suits you and works well for you. I did, and so can you.

Now, you need to get out there, back into your sales environment, and practice The Five Steps of the Sale. Watch the videos repeatedly. Listen to the audio series in your car, when walking along the beach, or practically anywhere else. Listen to it in your sleep, if you have to. Listen to it underneath a coconut tree, a mango tree, or any other tree of your liking. Wherever you are, listen to it.

Remember, practice, practice, and practice some more. Until next time, cheerio!

About the Author

Born in Kingston, Jamaica, Paul moved to the United States when he was 14 years old. The first place he called home in this country was the Bronx, NY. At the age of 17, he joined the U.S. Navy and reached the level of First Class Petty Officer.

In 1996, he moved to Orlando, FL, where he worked as a recruiter for the Navy, while also teaching 170 other recruiters how to excel and be top producers. Paul relocated to South Florida and started his real estate practice in 2003, selling more than 80 billion dollars in sales volume and developing a high-performance business owners coaching company.

Owing to his coaching, his clients have become top producers, succeeding in whatever they choose to do. Paul's clients have consistently said that they have opened doors to new ways of thinking, creativity, and problem-solving.

Since 1993 Paul has been practicing his unique selling technique and closing 99% of his presentations. Paul has continued to rank in the top 1% nationally for closing sales in multiple organizations. His tenacity of a bulldog mindset allows him to latch on his prospects and easily take them to a smooth closing. Does it sound amazing? Well, I'll let you answer that. In Paul's case, though, he has been using this system since 1993, to sell just about anything you can think of. The system is fun, vibrant, precise, logical, and, among other things, easy to learn.

No matter what product or service you have to offer, get ready to increase your sales closings by up to 10 times once you start using The Five Steps of the Sale. In most examples and contexts, Paul uses a real estate selling environment or atmosphere to get the point across. All you need to do is place yourself and your career or product in its place to understand the point.

He is a Published Author to the First real estate agent pocket guidebook, The Art & Science of The Real Estate Agent. Paul inspires, motivates, and provide services that cause an individual or group to gain High Producing levels. Most important, people are experiencing new learning, and changing the way they think.

Printed in the United States
by Baker & Taylor Publisher Services